I0437191

The Good Black Woman

The Good Black Woman

Palesa Pitso

Copyright © 2012 by Palesa Pitso.

| ISBN: | Softcover | 978-1-4797-1917-4 |
| | Ebook | 978-1-4797-1918-1 |

All rights reserved. No part of this book may be reproduced or transmitted in any form or by any means, electronic or mechanical, including photocopying, recording, or by any information storage and retrieval system, without permission in writing from the copyright owner.

This book was printed in the United States of America.

To order additional copies of this book, contact:
Xlibris Corporation
0-800-644-6988
www.xlibrispublishing.co.uk
Orders@xlibrispublishing.co.uk
304910

CONTENTS

Acknowledgements

With special thanks:

To all my friends for their support and those that urged me to carry on after having read and edited my book especially Phila Ngidi, Nontokozo Mkhize and Yolanda Sineke. May God bless you.

To Nompumelelo Dludla my pillar of strength, you always give me direction because you know me so well. God bless you my friend abundantly.

To Mbali Hlatshwayo who came right on time to give me the support I require. Thank You Mhayise.

To my only son Kwasa Khoza, who half the time never knew what I was getting up early for until I told him I have finished writing a book. You are a blessing in my life.

To my family, the Pitso's, at some point someone had to write a book, I guess it had to be me. I love all of you.

To Jabulani Mabaso, though we are not friends anymore, I thank you for suggesting that I write a book. You saw what I did not see in me, and it took 4 years for me to complete what I started in Cape Town. Thank You.

To the Xlibris publishers who gave me an incredible package and made my dreams a reality.

To all the Good black women out there, keep on believing in your abilities to shine and be the best that you can be without compromising yourself. Your struggles, desires, and joys do not go unnoticed by God. He will smooth your paths and calm your storms, and carry your loads. That is why I love Him so much.

The Preface

Many books have been written about woman but not particularly good black women except maybe in Biographies.

My book addresses the good black woman in General, no celebrity stuff, just the day to day life of a good black woman.

The title can be very confusing when you read on but that's exactly what I want each and every reader to be: Confused . . . . . but later you will understand what I am talking about

Why Good and why Black?

- Good is an Adjective that can mean different things to different people, it replaces other much more weighty adjectives such as Outstanding, Excellent, Fabulous etc
- Good is having admirable, pleasing, superior, or positive qualities. (Col Dict)
- Good means morally excellent, virtuous, righteous, suitable or efficient for a purpose.

I can go on and on describing the word Good . . . .

Good is just good.

Black is symbolic to me in the following way:

- Ethnically I am black but also African

- Black may denote a Race for people whose skin colour ranges from light to darker shades of Brown. Interesting! (Wilkemedia)
- In Western fashion Black creates a stylish, sexy, and powerful fashion statement
- Several bad incidents have been named Black e.g.. Black Thursday, Black Friday, Black December, Black November etc
- I live in a country where people are sensitive to being called black, others are confused as to whether they are black or not
- Black symbolizes secrecy, ambiguity or the unknown e.g.. Black market, Black magic, Blackmail etc

Black is just Black.

The book intends to highlight the challenges that are faced by all Good black women, I get into their minds, their bodies, their souls and in their lives, be it Church life, Married Life, Family life etc.

The book looks at good black women now and is aimed at being interesting to read five to ten years from now on.

Life has definitely changed for every Good black women, there are so many liberties and yet so many constraints. This is rhetoric, as the 'new independent woman generation' does not apply across the board. There is so much competition to succeed in the corporate world such that other things are compromised i.e. the family, children, relationships, time to play, etc

On the other hand the not so corporately independent sistas do not experience any liberties; life to them is just the same as 10 or 15 years ago.

If this book sparks controversy, so be it, its different strokes for different folks,

I SAY READ ON . . .

CHAPTER ONE

The Good Black Woman's Mystery: Men

Decide to be happy today, and to live with what is yours
(Author—unknown)

I bet every good black woman has read every book and every article about men. The "How To" and the "When to" books have graced every women's bookshelves, whether in the form of a Magazine, Paperback, Newspaper or Internet article, it has been read. Whether it's Mars, Hormones or Genes, our brothers continue to be a mystery. We love them, we adore them, we idolize them, we mother them and yet they are still a mystery to the Good black women.

Why do our brothers remain such an elusive entity . . . .?

Simple, they are made in Gods image. From Eden to Mars men will always continue to exist but will always be a mystery. They will do "good" things and "bad" things to those they proclaim to love . . . . for a reason . . . of course. A man doesn't do something for no reason and that is supposed to make everything bearable.

Let's see, the . . . . Reason can turn out in two ways . . . . (1)It will make a Good black woman strong or (2) It will shatter her. Whatever the case the reason will always be there, whether we like it or not.

How a man looks or views a good black woman today . . .

An equal rights fanatic, who knows her rights from bedroom to boardroom. A control freak who wants to remote control his whereabouts. A grammar phone always yapping about this and that. A school girl bedroom mate . . . . no action and no creativity whatsoever. What you saw body wise is just what you saw . . . . and not what you get out of your manly imagination. A woman is a silent successful competitor whose there to remind men of what they could have achieved had they lived "without" them. A reminder that she is not the only one of her kind but there are many like her, more beautiful, brainier and more 'woman". Cynical? Nope! Some men go to the extent of thinking about death even when death is not at the doorstep. The "she only wants my money syndrome" or when I am dead "she will spend my money with other fools" mentality is so much a factor in today's relationships more than ever before.

What a man needs to know about a good black woman . . .?

A Man needs to know that a good black woman is independent yes, but she is also vulnerable.

She is not an equal rights fanatics but she would like to be respected in all aspects of her human and women rights.

She is not a control freak but she would like to know your whereabouts because she loves you and because she cares about you, therefore she worries about you. She wants no harm to come your way!

Motherly? Yes, that's why we have maternal feelings.

If men would let them into their worlds there would be no time to ask thousands of questions about this and that. What is normally called communication break down is just Pride to let the other into the others world. What is wrong with telling a Good black woman that you will be late or that some friend is in need?

Is it right for a Good black woman to always wonder where you are, what you are doing with whom? Guess not because one day if you ever go missing it will be a Good black woman who has to answer.

I don't need a man to make me happy . . . .!!

The "I don't need a man attitude" portrayed by most good black women is actually Fandangle (nonsense), an Act. Every good black woman I know longs for companionship, love, understanding and acknowledgement from a partner. Even if the men are there to fix light bulbs, and lift heavy stuff, they are still needed.

The Car, the Town house, a child, parents, further education and designer clothes do not fill the void of loneliness at night, at parties, in concerts, and if I may add, at church.

However, this does not necessarily mean that sistas are in a mission to snatch any man that comes along nor are they eager to walk down the isle with just anyone . . . . I mean anyone!

A Good black woman is comfortable to be in the skin she is in, she has self worth, pride, dignity and there can be no other like her! When you see her, remember that!

Finally, the Educated and Financially secure Good black sistas are not there to remind men of their shortcomings nor are they in a position to pay all their accounts. Some of these women happen to have been fortunate enough to grow up believing in themselves and believing that a man's place is to be the provider, forget the sharing part for now!

A man is a Provider socially, religiously and ancestrally!!!

CHAPTER 2

A good black woman's Aspirations: Normalcy/Normality

No one owes you anything, if someone does something stupid or hurtful by your definition, just forgive and forget, life goes on

(Unknown—author)

Every Good black woman has aspirations about one thing or another. Aspirations are a good measure of success, whether achievable or just pipe dreams. You aspire to have a house, to get an education, to buy a car, to have a committed partner, to have kids or to get a well paying job. Simply put, aspiration is a strong desire to achieve something, such as success. Collins Dictionary

It took me a few days to come up with concrete thoughts around the word normal. I cracked my forehead trying to visualize normal, what is normal or rather who is normal?

After pondering on the subject for a while I realized that normal can be normal in a normal society and normal can be abnormal in an abnormal society.

Whatever your thoughts about normalcy and society—a good black woman aspires for normality in her life.

What does aspiring for normalcy look like?
Our society has the following social aspects:

- Working Women
- Single Parenting
- Infidelity
- Cohabiting
- Parenting

Normality is like chasing a dream with no ending. What is happening today won't guarantee a tomorrow. All Good black women in a quest to find normality have to contend with the above social realities and responsibilities.

A Good black woman has tried her best to balance everything from back in the olden days, from carrying a child on her back, a 20 litre bucket on her head, to carrying a bag in one hand. The trend is still there; women take everything, accommodate everyone and raise children.

The world is full of working women, who are mothers and worse than before, there are many single mothers than married moms. Being a working woman and a mother is not easy, it is even worse when you are a single parent, because you have to be everything to the children and bare the financial responsibility. It is not easy to do everything and pay for everything alone! Really.!

When single you find yourself wishing that there could be someone to assist you by taking care of one or two things in your life. Some parts of your life.

However at the end of it all, you get satisfaction when your child smiles and looks at you with those innocent eyes. It is such a Joy you would not trade for anything or anyone.

Singlehood challenges . . . . Men!

A Good black woman can also be a contradiction to her own values as tough times and moments are ever so increasing and sometimes when there is no solace, comfort can be begotten in sinful situations . . .

Whilst caught between being busy climbing the corporate ladder of success and sometimes parenting, then some boss sexually or physically harasses her because of her vulnerabilities and her need for financial stability knowing very well that the desperate circumstance will lead to desperate actions. Some men have studied the desperate women to the T. They know which buttons to touch to solicit a response, and most often than not, it is the dangling of money. The fact that there's no husband makes it even worse a Good black woman become an easy target to some preying male boss or preying financially mature man. In some instances the single woman becomes a full time mistress dating a married man.

Call it financial Stability or Mis-stress!

Almost every Good black woman is working or earning some kind of income, however this income becomes nothing when faced with a generous married man.

Why do so many married men have mistresses or office or social flings with mainly single women? Why do good black women succumb to be relegated to being the second best? It is not about Love definitely, no sane man would leave his wife for a fling termed love!!No! No! It could be financial stability on the side of the Good black woman or the feeling of getting attention from something forbidden.

However, the other woman may be regarded as an easer of stress or a stress releaser, hence mis-stress by someone's husband. Most Good black women mistresses began their relationships during the day in between corporate meetings and mostly on weekends during resting escapades.

My point is Good Black Single working women are vulnerable and sometimes susceptible to cunning men who want to relieve stress. And then again some Good black women enjoy this unsolicited attention because there is no one showing admiration, appreciation or consideration for their roles at home and at work. Some men sometimes think they are doing a Good black woman a favour especially when the woman is single.

Let us face it, every one wants to be admired and appreciated, and both these aspects are a large contributing fact to one's internal, motivational self worth or self esteem. That is why you will tend to find most Good black women comfortable with the role of being a Mis-stress.

Cohabiting

Every Good black woman was brought up in the knowledge that living with someone out of wedlock is a sin. It is something horrific and abominable such that when you are in your Teens you feel disgusted when you hear that so and so are living together for **Free.** You think of that washing, cooking, ironing, cleaning for a person for free and you feel it is all so sinful, horrendous and wrong.

However, most Good Black Women think and feel differently once they get into their 20s. I am saying 20s on purpose because the 20s are a dangerous age whereby most women feel and think different about things they thought and felt different about when they were teenagers. I t is much worse when they are in their 30s !

Cohabiting has many 'reasons', it has, we love each other, we want to get to know each other better before marriage, we sort of putting our eggs in one basket, and other reasons. The bottom line is there are reasons why people cohabit.

My opinion is, it is just a means to an end, whatever the means and whatever the end!!It's about a sense of belonging and a sense of not being lonely, period!

Whether the partner is responsible, loving, cheating, or whatever . . . the bottom line is, the partner is there and every Good black woman loves the feeling of not being alone.

How do you Parent children when there is all of the above?

A Good Black woman's Parenting skills are always under the spot light. Children are exposed to many social ills, on the television, in the internet, at school, at home and in society in general.

Ironically, many murders, rape, drug dealers, sexual addicts and abusers were once children of mothers who either worked or stayed at home.

All I know is that a Good black woman will always do the best for her children without reading from a 'How To" book. Parenting comes naturally, that desire to protect, to nurture, to guide and to compromise goals for your children comes from within.

It is however a challenge to raise children whilst society is giving information freely to kids and exposure to these social evils is so rampant.

However, Good black women are given children but children belong to God and a parent can only do so much in instilling good moral values to children. The bible is the cornerstone of the parenting it has all rules of raising future men and future wives. It also has warnings such as spare the rod and spoil the child which to some Good black woman can be confusing.

Be it as it may every Good black woman would continue raising their children the best way they know how, despite the social ills mentioned.

CHAPTER 3

A Good Black Woman's Exit: Marriage

Every exit is an entry somewhere else
—Tom Stoppard, an American dramatist

So many of the Good Black women grow up believing in the power of Marriage, not just any ones marriage but the power of their own marriage and a happy one at that.

No Good Black Woman ever dreams of a dreary life, full of unhappiness and boredom.

The picture of marriage in most Good black women's heads is that of pure marital bliss. Surely there can never be an unhappy person in a marriage after so much Monetary Transactions before, during and sometimes after the wedding day, that is the thought in most Good black women's minds.

In looking at the journey of marriage a Good black woman makes a sacrifice (NOT A GOOD WORD) and marry into another's family, she changes her Surname, inherit another's Family, habits, rituals and all, this clearly happens after being in her own family, and also being exposed to her own family's habits, rituals and all for many years. Picture that!!

Why the Sacrifice?

It could be a number of reasons: a sense of belonging, completing a mind picture or puzzle, seeking fulfillment, escaping a bad childhood, seeking justice, wanting children, others would say it is the right thing to do, or because her partner wanted to get married; I can think of a number of reasons but will concentrate on the one that stands out, that of Love. I would like to honestly and truthfully believe that Good black woman use marriage as an exit to attain happy ever after love.

What is loving a person?

Loving a person is difficult because it is not like loving a piece of cloth, shoes, a bag or chocolate slab. The latter you can have anytime you like, in whatever shape, colour or make and in whatever wrap or form, it cannot talk back or look at you because it's an IT—a thing. In the latter part of the century Love has come to mean a lot of things for different people, it is about wealth, social standing, and a friendship gig completion (my friends are married so should we).

These days' people get married because friends are married to Bee people the new in Term of the 20th century.

A **person** is a **human being** a descendant of the **Homo sapiens species.** I would like to draw your attention to this 3 in 1 definition—what does this mean exactly?

An online site called the Dictionary.com defines a Person as a living human, the composite of characteristics that make up an individual personality, the self. It further states that a person's physique and general appearance, an individual human being whether man, woman, or child. And that a person is an individual human being, especially with reference to his or her social relationships and behavioral patterns as conditioned by the culture.

Notice the use of human being in defining a person. Now let us look at human being.

The online Oxford Dictionaries defines Human being as a man, woman, or child of the species Homo sapiens, distinguished from other animals by superior mental development, power of articulate speech, and upright stance.

Homo Sapiens is derived from Latin whereby Homo means "wise man" or "knowing man").When compared to other animals and primates, humans have a *highly developed brain*, capable of *abstract reasoning*, *language*, *introspection* and *problem solving*.

The above definitions explain why it has to be difficult to love a person, who is also a human being and a Homo Sapien.

In other words it tells us that you love someone who has his/her own characteristics that form an individual personality which is called the self. The self is composed of the physical and general appearance distinguishing one from an animal or thing and further conditioned by social and behavioral aspects of culture.

A wise man/woman or knowing man/woman who has a highly developed brain, reasoning, language, introspection and problem solving abilities.Phew!

This clearly indicates that for two to become one in Marriage there clearly has to be leverage between two persons. On the other hand it also explains why it is difficult to understand and love another gender because we are different and unique made of different compositions.

One of the the things that cause man and women to be unique is the way we were raised by different parents. We developed certain habits and traits that make out a different composition of who and what we are that by the time you meet your better half you are already a composition of two persons: what you grew up knowing from your parents and what you discovered in the world by yourself.

How do you bring such diverse people together into one? Husband and wife.

If you think about it marriages do not fail on their own. It is a challenge to find a mate that is why most Good Black women have to go through a series of mates before they can get married to the One. So many individuals possess so many qualities and traits that sometimes even the One may not be the One.

The diverse nature of a person can cause confusion in that you may think you know them very well for a month or two, only to find out down the line you are dealing with a completely new person who also thinks that you have changed and thus a series of negative emotions can thus emanate from the fact that both of you are **persons.**

CHAPTER 4

A Good Black Woman's Worst Nightmare: Divorce

Those who honestly mean to be true contradict themselves more rarely than those who try to be consistent
—Oliver Wendell Holmes Jr an American Jurist

Every good black woman does not dream about divorce, actually it's a nightmare that one never thinks of when they marry.

The actual thought of letting go of your spouse, the material things, dividing assets into two and even deciding where the kids would go is tearing up inside, it's the worst nightmare. It is something one will tread carefully when deciding on.

However, the stark reality is that a Good black woman does get divorced or divorces for reasons beyond her control. Some of the reasons might be that the spouse is cheating, and despite the family's pleas that she must stay in the marriage because every man cheats so she should stay, the Good black woman decides "once a cheater, always a cheater" and thus files for divorce. Perhaps it's the verbal and physical abuse that despite counseling it never ends. In some instances the Good black woman might choose the divorce route because of what those that are learned call "irreconcilable differences" and, mind you, they mean just that—irreconcilable.

This brings back again what I mentioned in Chapter 3 about bringing two persons together in marriage. What does it entail? What becomes so different and so unbearable in marriage?

Differences in your upbringing in relation to money matters—you are a miser and I am not, therefore you tend to control my spending. Arguments and differences of opinion will always be about how money should be spent. No two couples can have the same spending patterns. The way one is brought out has a bearing later in life and would show in spending patterns. Most Good black woman find themselves in such similar arguments about money and the latter is the largest contributor in divorce.

Differences in raising children—at home we were spanked and you were not, therefore my children will grow up the same way. Most Good black women would like to raise their children the way they were raised. However most often than not disagreements on child rearing will always prevail as each one would like to instill discipline that is different to the other. In some instances the Good black woman will have to contend with a spouse that does not discipline children at all but criticizes her methods of child rearing.

Differences about religion—I am from this church and you are from this one and therefore since this is my house you will go to my church. Good black woman grow up going to their home churches. However, as soon as a Good black woman changes her surname, her church is supposed to change. Imagine knowing your church rituals for years and years and then later in life you learn new hymns and new church rituals. Some Good black woman adjust to the change, most negotiate, And win, but for most there is no compromise thus the latter results to dire penalties and consequences which end up in a nightmare.

Differences in raising children born before marriage—your kid will stay with your mom I don't want them here; I cannot raise another woman's child. This is a sore thorn on the side as children born outside of marriage suffer mostly as spouses fight over them. Most Good black women do not accept children born out of wedlock especially if they are forced on them. The other side of the coin is that most good Black women would accept illegitimate children if they do not discover that the father is still seeing the mother in clandestine conditions. The other children are not a problem to the Good black woman, but the problem is how they are introduced into the marriage. The problem is founding out that they are kept a secret. The problem is that the baby mama calls at anytime. The problem is that there is not only one child, but two, three or four that were not declared before marriage. The problem is that, even after the marriage there are new children being born out of wedlock. This nightmare eventually leads to divorce

Differences in just about everything—how the colour of the house should be blue, the furniture should be antique and where the house should be bought, what car is suitable for the family, what make, and so on, mhmm a bone of contention marriage seems to impose on everything. Again, I say, two people from different genes and from different environments who have their own dispositions made out of different compositions.

Why is it so easy to argue and difficult to resolve arguments? Such is the diverse nature of relationships and especially marriage where there are sacred vows.

All the Good black woman who have come across the above have been faced with the difficulty of facing divorce, questions like: If I leave, what about the children, what about the church, parents, the society and house finances, are sometimes difficult to answer, hence most Good black women end up staying in loveless marriages.

Married Good black women do not want to leave their spouses for they love them but when the love is gone and when there is no compromise nor a solution to some of the issues, and then they choose the option of divorce.

CHAPTER 5

A Good black woman's Taboo: Sexuality and Change

Men believe that a society is disintegrating when it can no longer be pictured in familiar terms. Unhappy is a people that has run out of words to describe what is going on
—Thurman Arnold, an American Lawyer

Every good black woman knows their sexual orientation from birth. I am using the word orientation for a reason.

Orientation means: a person's awareness of self with regard to position and time and place and personal relationships,

Sexual Orientation means you are aware of your sexuality by the way your organs are positioned from birth and then act accordingly.

You become orientated to your sexuality through your genitalia, your family calling you boy or girl and society being able to assimilate the latter.

However, sexual orientation does not define your feelings from birth and when you grow up. You can have a woman's body but feel different and experience different sexual feelings about yourself towards other women, not that it changes the fact that you are still woman.

What prompts the need for the same sex relationship?

Connectivity, fashion, denial, disappointments or just pure love that makes good black women want to have relationships with their fellow good black woman. Let us examine each;

Connectivity and the good black woman mean 3cs: companionship, chemistry, and crying. Woman to Woman relationships are characterized by connectivity, laughing at the same jokes together, going to the same parties, watching the same movies, having common friends and enjoying the sex. However, with time this collapses as it was based on connectivity rather than love, true love and so this leads to crying, buckets of tears at that.

Fashion is a fool's paradise mentality, whereby people imitate whatever they think and feel is "IN" at that particular point in time. Woman to Woman relationships are sometimes characterized by "It looks nice, everybody is doing it and so can I" mindset. This good black woman stance is a disaster as it sometimes leads to undefined roles, expectations and too much bickering and again there is no sound foundation to make the relationship sustainable. Fashion is seasonal and fashion eventually passes.

Have you ever had a feeling of something nagging your conscience every day, the only time its quiet is when you are asleep. When you open your eyes in the morning it comes back again, you carry it throughout the day until you go to bed at night. Even when you pray about it, fast about it and talk about it, it just would not go away. Painful thing! Pretending something is not there is the worst thing a good black woman can do to herself.

Denial is some characteristic of Woman to Woman relationships whereby a person is defined by society's expectations and they choose to live a double life. Having feelings for the same sex person is not something new and being in denial about it makes matters worse. Love thy neighbor as thy self can also encompass loving another woman. If such is denied to exist it will turn to be like a disease, if left on its own, it can eat at you until you become just a fragmentation of your true self.

Disappointments with man can result in good black women seeking solace and adventure on their counterparts. Life does not always turn out to be what we envisage it to be. Every Good black woman grows up thinking they will all become happily married mothers, with two children, a boy and a girl. This picture grows in one's mind and forms a bigger picture that all will be hunky dory and all fairytale. However, life teaches one to jump from one relationship to the next forming a cycle in a bid to try and find the perfect partner in order to complete the picture that existed in the mind from the puberty stage.

After much trying with no success, some Good black women seek peace in another woman's arms. This turn in relationship preferences for some guarantees, respect, honesty, laughter, and fun times.

However, this is a dangerous zone to tread on because it cannot be maintained when a good guy comes along.

Lastly, let me delve on Pure Love for this one is next to my heart in so many ways. We sometimes meet people by chance, sometimes we are introduced to them and sometimes we meet them out of other circumstances. Whatever the situation, we meet people regardless of how and why. People always say everything happens for a reason, I believe them even when I don't know if that reason ever comes out.

Pure love in women to women relationships exists, it is that feeling that you carry with you day in and day out. It is that feeling that makes you miss a person even when you have just spoken to them. It is that feeling that makes you want to see a person even when you have just seen them. It is the warmness of the heart when you think about that person. It is the sparkle in your eyes and a smile on the face each time you think about that special person. It is feeling comfortable about anything and anyone when you have won that special Good black woman. It is knowing that whatever happens that person will stand by you through thick and thin. It is about knowing you have a friend, a partner, an advisor, a mentor and a sister in one person and feeling like telling the whole world about it.

It is being able to forgive several times without counting how many times. It is about bearing your soul and loving without expecting anything in return. It is about honesty, respect, caring, protecting and giving without making an effort, as these come naturally.

Mostly it is the peace that you feel with that person, peace that resonates within you and transcends all else.

Pure love is indeed a rare find even in Woman to Woman relationships, it is what a good black woman should treasure and should keep forever until death separates.

Pure love can only be the foundation for **the same sex relationship.**

CHAPTER 6

A good black woman's Anger: Betrayal

Where all think alike, no one thinks very much
—Walter Lippmann, an American Journalist

There is nothing explosive like a Good black woman betrayed. Betrayal in the eyes of a woman could mean different things depending on the issue one feels strongly about. In its simple forms betrayal could mean:

1. Being disappointed, proved undependable to; abandoned, forsaken
2. Being sexually unfaithful to one's partner in marriage
3. giving away information about somebody
4. causing someone to believe something that is untrue

Whatever you choose as your definition from the above, betrayal is being untrue to someone, simple.

Most good black women have encountered one or two forms of betrayal in their lifetime. Betrayal by a friend, a lover, spouse, family member or colleague. The anger associated with being betrayed is insurmountable and sometimes difficult to overcome and can be fatal at times.

Why do good black women betray each other?

The most profound aspects of betrayal are taking someone for granted. Most of the time we tend to not know what we have until it is not there anymore. We tend to not appreciate the people that love us the most until they are gone. We tend to bask in the delight of another's suffering forgetting that the wheel turns and what goes around may come around. Let us look at a few causes of Betrayal:

Boredom in ones life or in a relationship can lead to a person making rash decisions such as engaging in unsolicited gossip or engaging in multiple relationships. Running away from acknowledging that you are bored and trying to do something exciting can lead one astray. We all know that most extra marital affairs come as a result of boredom and chasing after fantasies.

Is it not easy to declare neither your boredom nor your fantasies to friends or colleagues. Every Good black woman wants to be seen as happy and living a delightful life. How then do we end up with Gossip mongers or cheaters if life so blissful for the Good black woman? The simplest solution for any Good black woman is to find something to do, rather than engage in backstabbing gossip, that extra relationship on the side and drama which at the end of the day is not worthwhile.

The second cause of betrayal can be linked to Greed, it is very easy for someone to be unsatisfied with what they have and long for something more, something that they do not have. Pining after someone's boyfriend, girlfriend, husband and longing for the items those friends possess. Greed begins from the eye, what you see makes you yearn for something that you do not have. Greed has seen friendships collapse and relationships destroyed. Greed causes unnecessary tension in any relationship. I have seen most Good black woman become enemies because of business ideas stolen from each other. Some "stealing" each other's lovers. A Good black woman besotted by greed does not live a joyful life at all.

Jealousy is the crux of every betrayal, especially if one is envious of another Good black woman's achievements. Friends can be susceptible to this kind of spiritual evil. The amount of time spent looking for differences, plotting to outdo the other and waiting for mistakes is just wasted energy. Good black women have destroyed each other through competition, negative competition in relationships, at work, happen through sabotages. Fighting to win friends, competition about fashion trends, instead of appreciating what the other has, you will find Good black women pulling each other down and getting buy in from other onlookers, who happen to be Good black women. Good black women can betray each other's trust through jealousy, which is such wasted energy.

Selfishness results in loneliness. Is this a fair statement? The more you are selfish is the more you alienate yourself from those you love and from people in general. Achieving things by selfish means can result in betrayal. Good black woman who have begotten things by selfish means have often lost those things. Remember the old adage which is a warning "do not envy your neighbour's belongings"

Insecurity is a killer of relationships. A good black woman, who has not learnt to love herself, be proud of whom she is, and to trust in her capabilities is dead alive. A good black woman cannot find security in betraying another that is living in a fool's paradise. Good black women have betrayed each other because of feeling in adequate, feeling that they do not belong, feeling like they do not fit and feeling like they are less of women than others. Good black women have been their worst enemies in this regard because, there is nothing worse than feeling insecure as it makes one do crazy things, some regrettable.

CHAPTER 7

A good black woman's fear: Loneliness

Almost anything is easier to get into than out of
—Agnes Allen, an American epigrammatist

Mhmm! In chapter 2 I mentioned that every good black woman aspires for something, education, a house, husband, loving partner, kids etc. Sadly no one aspires to be lonely, however the life that we are living is so unpredictable such that most black woman end up lonely.

The sad part about loneliness is finding most good black women who are terrified of being lonely clutching on to unhealthy relationships.

I need not mention that the more a good black woman stays in an unhealthy relationship the more difficult it is to let go. These relationships tend to cause more damage psychologically as they do not lead into anything constructive at the end.

The trend nowadays is that most learned good black women tend to go out with younger partners. Perhaps let us delve deep into the core of these relationships by examining two things; Loneliness and Loneliness.

Most often than not a good black woman will feel comfortable in a relationship whereby they have control. In most heterosexual relationships you find that the man is always in control of everything such that there is no room for negotiations or the changing of roles. Amazingly when a good black woman has managed to come out of a controlling relationship they want to control as well. So the easiest prey is a younger partner. Younger partners are submissive, dependant and sometimes loyal.

The other side of the coin of loneliness is when younger partners become demanding and manipulative preying on the insecurities of the older partner. They detect form the early stages of the relationship when they are given money, cars and taken out to fancy restaurants that they are being caged in. They will then start demanding things and on offer they ground themselves more into this tie until they are tired and they move on.

Loneliness can be a terrible feeling I agree, if you look at it as a death sentence. There are good black women who have sacrificed themselves, have lost their possessions in a bid to hold on to partners. The fear of being lonely is tantamount to being giving or rather bribery.

The loneliness can transcend to feelings of being insecure, irrational and clingy. Suffice to say that a good black woman who fears loneliness can be suffocating to their partners.

Not only do most Good black women fear to be ultimately abandoned by the men in their lives—they fear it from other women as well. They fear to be abandoned by friends, colleagues and their children when they grow up.

Most Good black women, believe it's shameful to be lonely, some begin to doubt themselves, more especially where relationships are concerned.

The issue of childhood wounds perhaps of a mother or a father abandoning the family, wounds that have not healed, may be linked to the feminine fear of loneliness. Perhaps the fear of leaving an unhealthy relationship comes from wanting to not do the same as the father did or what the mother did.

Perhaps the fear of facing family and society as a lonesome woman is a dreadful thought but not a dreadful circumstance.

At some point if things do not go the way they are planned, a Good black woman has to say "This is not worth it, let me go it alone" and from that point onward they will live and lead a healthier life.

CHAPTER 8

A good black woman's most dreaded disease: Hiv/Aids

I am not afraid of death. It's just that I don't want to be there when it happens

—Woody Allen, an American Actor

Every good black woman dreads the thought of being infected with the HIV virus. However, most have become victims of the scourge not as a result of their own doing but through their encounters with partners that already have the diseases or partners who went astray and got the disease elsewhere.

I cannot out rule the fact that most good black women have been infected with the virus because of not letting go of a relationship that was not bringing them any joy, and because of the fear of being lonely discussed in the previous chapter. Trusting a promiscuous partner and having sexual contact without protection is but a Good black woman's downfall. No person can stand between a Good black women and sexual gratification except herself.

Instances of sexual abuse and rape are but shameful to our society, and how can we be called normal in an abnormal society. These are but an exception for the Good black woman that has been infected through such heinous acts.

Many good black women have become victims of rape and sexual abuse and have thus contracted the virus unknowingly through no fault of their own.

Innocent victims are in the conscience of many who are infected but are still running around infecting others. Surprisingly infected women will seldom disclose their status to new partners for fear of being rejected and marginalized. It is much safer to keep quiet about it then being rejected and mocked. For many good black women being HIV positive is like carrying a big Iron cross with only one destination: Death.

It need not be so though, as everyone in this crazy world is carrying an Iron cross one way or another of some ailment or the other of some secret or of some burden. It is the way you deal with your cross that matters, running away from it would not solve the problem either. It is about understanding it, embracing it and living with it gracefully by educating and warning others to live responsible lives.

Responsible behavior comes from protecting oneself and your partner. I am ashamed that selfish behavior has caused some good black women not to protect their partners after they are diagnosed as HIV positive. I shudder at the thought that some good black women have the "I don't want to die alone ", or the "What if I get rejected "mentality. The world has become a dog eat dog fiasco, free sex is abundant and caution is not exercised.

A good black woman who loves herself and who knows that life is precious would not go on a spree of infecting others. Some good black women have gotten love; some have married because of their honesty to their partners about their status. I salute those women for their courage and for knowing that each and every person has a right to live.

After all the evils, unfairness, and the failed encounters the good black woman still needs and wants love.

CHAPTER 9

A good black woman's sanity: Healing

He that lacks time to mourn lacks time to mend.
William Shakespeare, an English dramatist

When all has been said and done, there follows the question, how does a good black woman find healing, for healing is but a process.

The good black woman lives in a society that merely knows much about healing. Therapy and Healing are but a Western phenomenon. Meanwhile families, friendships and partnerships are destroyed and there is no sense of closure in the form of healing. Most good black women tend to bury their hurt behind the words "I am fine" to maintain their "strong" status. What is fine?

Is it fine that being a good black woman you were once abused sexually, verbally or physically? Is it fine that most good black woman have lost friendships and associations because they betray one another? Is it fine that most good black woman cannot have healthy relationships because of their past pains with their parents, partners or friends? Is it fine to hate those who have hurt you? Is it fine to bury your sorrows in alcoholic drinks? Is it fine to jump from one relationship to the next as a form of escapism? What is fine?

So much of a Good black women's energy is spent on suppressing pain. This obsession of showing a brave face, keeping things together and yet inside a Good black woman is in pieces is prevalent in most Good black women. The brevity that knows no limits is the exact cause of so many psychiatric and neurological wards being full of Good black women because of depression and stress. Some argue that the latter are a "White man's disease", so much for passing the buck, I don't agree, in life you need to have coping mechanisms. Our parents suffered no such diseases because they found means of dealing with their stress by ploughing the field, by doing household chores, by going to church, by sitting around the fire or family table and told stories of hope.

The Good black women have to know that the journey to being fine begins with the first step and that is finding healing. How do you find healing?

1. Acknowledging your pain
2. Making sense of your pain
3. Categorizing your pain.
4. Understanding that your pain is meant for you only.
5. Learn and perhaps teach others about your pain if you must.

At the onset I am reminded of the Alabaster box bible story, whereby a woman that was seen to be unclean and impure touched Jesus by her actions. She was in so much pain and crying and Jesus did the unthinkable and embraced her, a Nobody.

It makes you wonder where all the tears of good black women go, tears of pain. Sometimes the pain we feel is necessary to make us stronger so that that we can manage to face the future with vigor. It is sometimes necessary so that we can lean closer to our maker. It is necessary so that we can be humble. It is necessary so that we can learn that other people are not like us. Other times it's not necessary, really.

Acknowledging your pain is admitting that you are hurting and that it is painful here . . . . *pointing*.Pretending that you are not hurting will not make the pain go away indefinitely; it's a temporal solution for a Good black woman trying to be brave.

After acknowledging your pain the next step is making sense of your pain. Do you think the pain is meant for you only or it was just unfortunate that you ended up being the victim? What are the events that led to the pain? Did you see the warning signs but chose to ignore them? Did you contribute to your pain somehow, one way or the other? What was your part in causing your own pain or in prolonging it? What have to learn in any case about this pain?

Does shutting the door of a painful room in our hearts, make things better or does it make the pain worse?

Does locking the pain away (the pain of rejection, betrayal, lost relationships and so on) and throwing the key, bring a sense of relief, perhaps for a while? The old adverb "of letting sleeping dogs lie", does it bring relief?

A Good black woman has to contend with such questions on her journey to healing.

Categorizing your pain, simple means breaking it down and deciding how long you intend staying with it. Is it going to be a long term, medium or short term pain? How are you going to deal with it going forward? Are you going to cry for twenty days for someone that left you for another partner or are you going to cry five days and decide to put the matter to rest because it will no longer be worth your tears.

Every good black women needs to streamline their pain accordingly. Sometimes we need not put every pain in an extreme pain shelf or a serious pain shelf. There are those things that you learn from, that you laugh about e.g. your foolishness that ended in you being hurt.

Understanding that your pain is meant for you only and not for someone else is a step towards healing. You will find that every black woman has once said "Why me"? this you ask when you are going through a difficult time. I ask, Why not you? Cry if you must but keep going because this particular pain that you are dealing through was meant for you and you only.

Learning and teaching others about your pain will best answer the question "Why me"? Sometimes we learn from our pain, from our foolishness and from our mistakes. Life is a school and we are the learners, for us to graduate from the school of life we have to be well taught to teach others to avoid pitfalls. If you tell others your story, that is another form of therapeutic healing, in some instances you will laugh at your own folly and in some instances you will cry at your own weaknesses and vulnerabilities and but the ultimate healing will be taking place. My story can be your story if you know about it, simple.

Be it as it may, every Good black woman has a painful story to tell . . . .

CHAPTER 10

Finally: A good black woman and her conscience

To exist is to change, to change is to mature, to mature is to go on creating oneself endlessly
—Henri Bergson, a French Philosopher

For the past two months I have been wondering what my closing chapter should be about until today (05/06/2011) when at church suddenly a voice gave me the word "conscience" and as my last chapter to this book I have to now come up with issues around this word.

Every good black woman has a conscience and if you are wondering whether you have one or not, yes you do. A conscience is that tiny little voice that tells you what is right and what is wrong and tell you to move away from trouble. It is that voice that makes us classify good versus bad. It is that voice that tells you it is not right to be in love with a married man or woman, or tells you not to cheat in your relationship; it will tell you when you are in the wrong relationship or the wrong company of friends. A conscience will tell you if you are neglecting your child or children, or if you are spending time on other things rather than on your parents, siblings or children.

Unfortunately every Good black woman has a conscience and unfortunately every Good black woman tends to ignore their consciences in favour of other bad choices and the latter causes them to live a guilt ridden life.

Wouldn't it be nice if every Good black woman would listen to their conscience that tells them to move away from an unhealthy relationship? Wouldn't it be nice if you would listen to the voice that tells you to forgive rather than to hate? Wouldn't it be nice to listen to the voice that tells you that you are not ok and that you need help? Wouldn't it be nice to listen to the voice that tells you not to run away from your problems but that you should stay and fight them? Wouldn't it be nice not to marry someone you know you don't love? Wouldn't it be nice to remind your partner to put on a condom for your sake and theirs before you engage in unprotected sexual intercourse? Wouldn't it be great if you were to tell your parents that you are attracted to people of your same gender rather than pretend you are in love with someone of the opposite sex?

Undoubtedly having a conscience can also be painful.

Almost every Good black woman is trapped in a life they are not supposed to be living as a matter of good principles. Most Good black woman are not living for themselves, however they are living for society in a world of "what would people say", some live for their parents in a world of "what would my parents say", some live for their kids "what would my kids say".

A cumbersome question is, when will a Good black woman begin to live for herself, do the things that she loves the most, living her dreams, be with someone she loves regardless of what people say.

Instead of moving forward healing ourselves of past wounds, we stay in unhealthy relationships because of fear of moving forward to another relationship.

Instead of finding a support group for our different ailments, we stay and wallow in self pity about the HIV status, or the sexual abuse or the physical abuse we suffered at our own expense.

Is the Good black woman dead yet? No. Then why are most Good black women living their lives as if they are mourning it?

When is the right time to start anew, to move forward, and to enjoy the rest of the life that God has given to us as a gift?

Having a conscience does not mean you must not enjoy the finer things in life. Every Good black woman is blessed with intuition "that tiny voice that tells you to stay clear of harm's way" without reasoning, listen to it before entering that relationship, or before making a drastic decision about your future.

Good black woman, you are beautiful, intelligent and are surrounded by family, and friends that love you. You are the epitome of the finest diamond ever carved from a jagged stone.

Love yourself and be content with who you are, do not seek validation form society, friends or from a partner for your very existence was validated by the most High.

Every Good black woman is Special in her own way.

www.ingramcontent.com/pod-product-compliance
Lightning Source LLC
Chambersburg PA
CBHW050348290526
45785CB00006B/2677